THE TONY HART
ART FACTORY

Happy Birthday
To Jennifer!

Much love,

Auntie Marianne
Uncle John
Helen Matthew & Francesca

TO ROC RENALS
WITH UNDIMINISHED ADMIRATION
THIS BOOK IS AFFECTIONATELY
DEDICATED

THE TONY HART
ART FACTORY

KAYE & WARD · LONDON

First published by Kaye & Ward Ltd
Century House, 82/84 Tanner Street, London SE1 3PP
1980

ISBN 0 7182 1262 2

Printed in Great Britain by
The Fakenham Press Ltd, Fakenham, Norfolk

Introduction

There could be some muttering in the Schools of Fine Arts that the words 'art' and 'factory' should be used in the same breath. No matter; art is human skill or workmanship. A factory is a place of manufacture. This book is intended for anyone with average human skill to design and manufacture pictures. Most of these are similar to those shown on my television programmes. That you, too, wish to make pictures along these lines has been made abundantly clear from the sacks full of letters that reach me.

In this book I have limited the art projects to twelve areas. From these areas I think you will find something that appeals to your particular talent or interest. These areas are: stencils, printing and sand art; inks, wax and paper; metal, light and patterns; stone, markers and rubbings. Well over a hundred art forms for you to create. Most people, especially children, have a natural sense of design and will experiment with colour, shape and line to create something exciting and satisfying. Perhaps my suggestions will spark off your enthusiasm. The materials recommended will cost you very little and can be found in most households.

I know that many teachers, Group Leaders and Art and Craft Societies have found my ideas useful – a tremendous compliment. I hope that they, and also the children, and the retired people will go on to produce further ideas of their own. The scope is unlimited.

It is specially helpful to look at everything with more than a passing interest. See what happens to buildings, pavements and streets under different lighting conditions. Look at the patterns of brickwork and the texture of man-made materials. In the country there is the pattern of growing things: tree bark, plants, leaves and grasses. Dead wood can be particularly beautiful. All these things should be observed closely. You might be inspired to make a design after studying sawn logs, or having looked at a pebble under a magnifying glass. I promise you'll get more out of life if you do. And when you are inspired to create, there are dozens of mediums for you to work in. Observe and experiment and enjoy it.

Contents

TERMS USED IN THIS BOOK

ABSTRACT	Design that exists only in the mind
ADHESIVE	Any sort of glue or sticking substance
ASSEMBLAGE	Any chunky materials put together to form a whole
DESIGN	Any decorative, planned drawing
GLOSS	Any paint or ink that shines when dry
HIEROGLYPH	A drawing used to represent a word or sound
IMPRESS	Pressing into clay to obtain a pattern
MATT	Opposite of gloss
MEDIA	(Plural of Medium) Materials which you choose to work in, i. e. paint, clay, ink, etc.
MOSAIC	A picture made up from a number of tiny, similar units
PATTERN	A design in which some features are repeated
REPRESENTATIONAL	A picture in which the objects can be recognised as they are
SGRAFFITO	Scratching on or into a surface
SIMULATE	To assume the appearance of something else
STYLISED	Recognisable, but not representational
TEXTURE	The surface of objects that can be felt, i. e. glass, stone, cloth

SUPPLIERS

(If you have difficulty in obtaining from local stockists)

WAX CRAYONS	Harbutt's Plasticine Ltd, Bathampton, Bath
PLASTICINE	Harbutt's Plasticine Ltd, Bathampton, Bath
MODELLING CLAY	Newday Products Ltd
PAPER	Hunt & Broadhurst Ltd, Ideal Works, Vatley Road, Oxford
SPECIALISED PAPER	Paperchase, 213 Tottenham Court Road, London W1
METAL FOIL	Stuart Aluminium, Penn Road, Wolverhampton
ADHESIVES (Latex) (Universal) (Wallpaper Paste)	Copydex Ltd, 1 Torquay Street, London W2 Unibond Ltd, Tuscan Way, Camberley, Surrey Polycell Ltd, Broadwater Road, Welwyn Garden City, Herts.
GENERAL MATERIALS (Paints, inks, brushes, papers, markers, etc.)	Geo. Rowney & Co, PO Box 10, Bracknell, Berks. Reeves & Son, Lincoln Road, Enfield, Middlesex Windsor & Newton, Wealdstone, Harrow, Middlesex
PLASTER OF PARIS	Most chemists
PLASTER	DIY Shops or Builders Merchants

Stencils, prints
and sand art

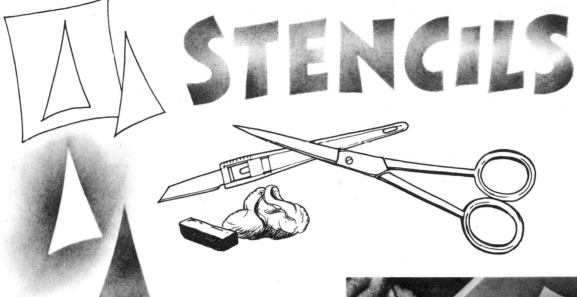

STENCILS

Cut stencils with craft knife or scissors. Use chalk powder and cotton wool.

Use cartridge paper or thin card for stencils and masking pieces. Draw round coin, or use compass, to help make wavy line.

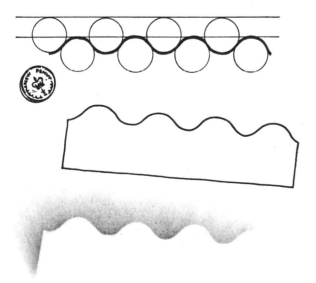

A 'stubber' is made from tightly rolled blotting paper or newsprint.

Make a pointed end and use to obtain this effect.

Stipple brush

Foam rubber used with ink or paint can be dabbed over stencil.

Aerosol spray

'Blow it yourself' spray (Diffuser)

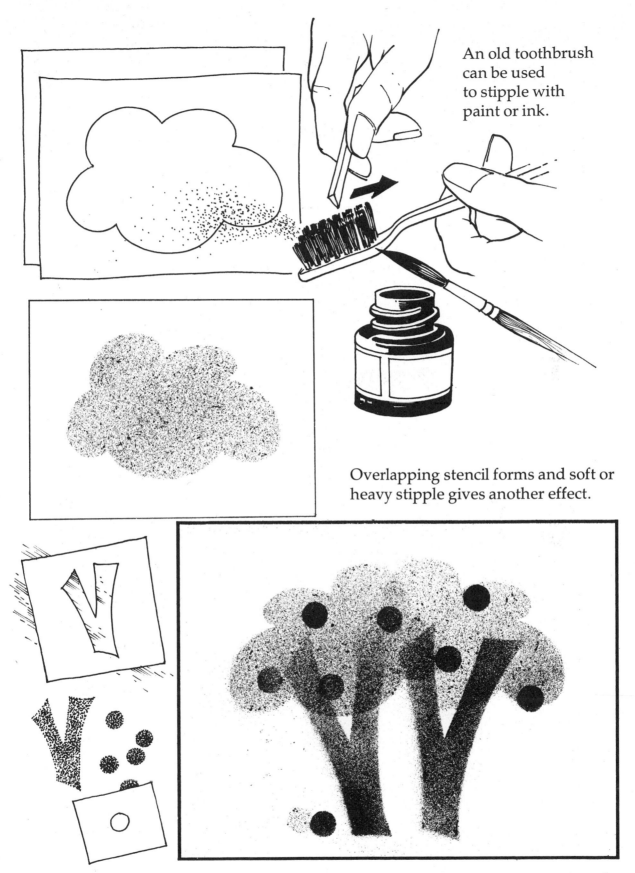

An old toothbrush
can be used
to stipple with
paint or ink.

Overlapping stencil forms and soft or
heavy stipple gives another effect.

The face here could easily be made into a stencil. It has
been traced from a photograph. Only the dark areas
have been drawn. When these are filled in the face
becomes very real. We need no more information.

If you want to enlarge the drawing, it helps if you square it up. Prepare a sheet of paper with larger squares and copy what is in each small square into each larger square. The areas to be filled in can be painted an overall colour, or can be filled with patterns or even bits cut from a magazine. (See colour plate.)

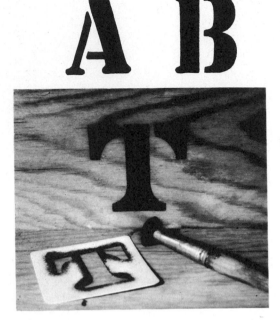

If you cut out letters for stencilling remember that the middle will fall out of some letters like 'O'. You have to leave a bridge to hold the middle in. Some letter stencils leave bridges in even when they're not needed to keep the design looking the same.

The bits you cut out of a stencil can be used as a mask. The used masks and stencils make interesting collages.

The artist Toulouse Lautrec used
paper masks when stippling his
lithographs.

Stencils and masks have been used
over and over again to make this
picture. See how effective it is to
make things look round.

PRINTS and PRINTING

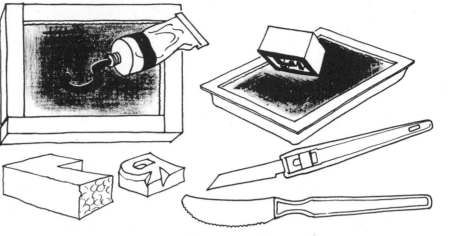

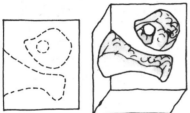

Polystyrene is good for making blocks from which to print. Young children can use plastic picnic knives for cutting, or even pick away at a polystyrene rectangle to make a block for repeat patterns.

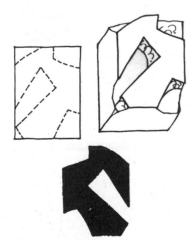

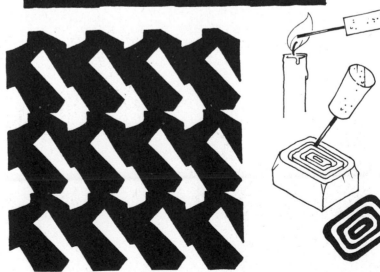

A nail, held in a cork, when heated will melt polystyrene. Useful for detailed blocks.

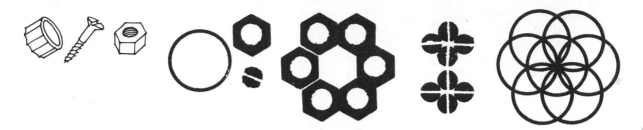

Prints from a bottle top, a screw and a steel nut.

Start with a square. Anything cut from one side must be stuck to the opposite edge with glue.

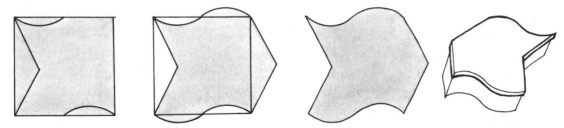

If you make a cardboard block this way you can make a satisfying repeat pattern.

The bird and the cat's head have been worked out this way. (See colour picture on page **1.**16).

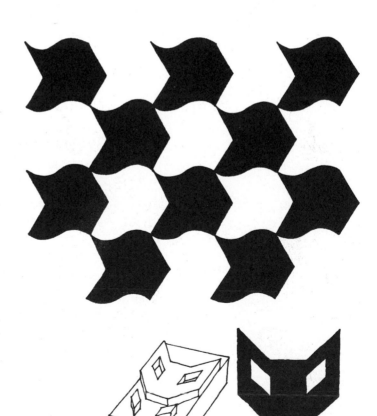

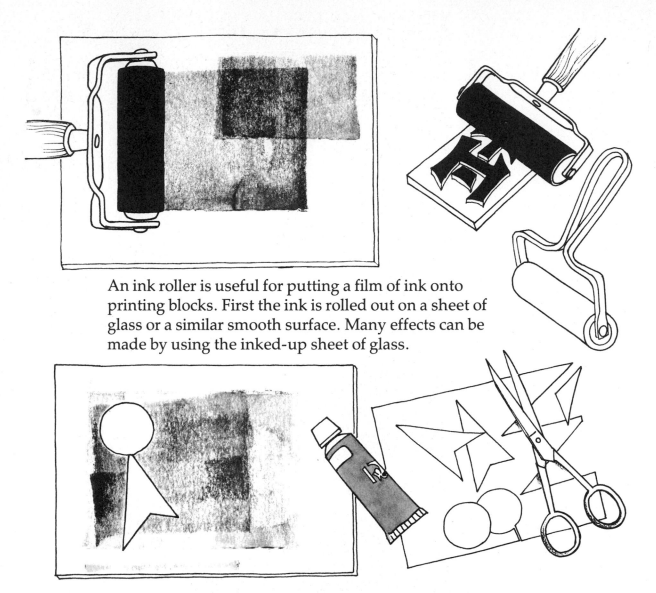

An ink roller is useful for putting a film of ink onto printing blocks. First the ink is rolled out on a sheet of glass or a similar smooth surface. Many effects can be made by using the inked-up sheet of glass.

Try cutting out paper shapes and laying them on the inked surface. Lay a sheet of thin paper on top. Rub with the palm of the hand. Peel off the paper. This is a monoprint. You can only do it once!

The head was cut
out of paper and
used as a mask,
lightly stuck to
cartridge paper. A
printing roller inked
up with black ink is
rolled over both
papers, then the
masking paper is
removed. The
second colour, or
tone, is made by
printing from one
polystyrene block.

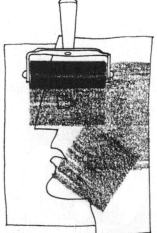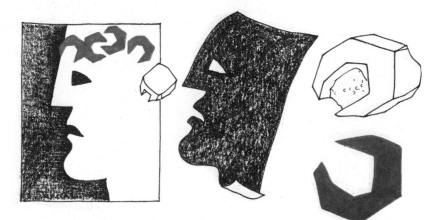

Mask

You can take the monoprint a stage further. After the paper has been removed with the monoprint, the masking paper is stuck to the inked-up glass sheet. If you peel off the masking paper you can then make a second, quite different print from the glass sheet. The large picture on this page shows the sort of result.

Monoprint

Remove mask

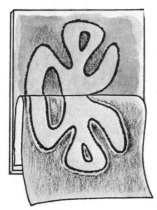

Make second print

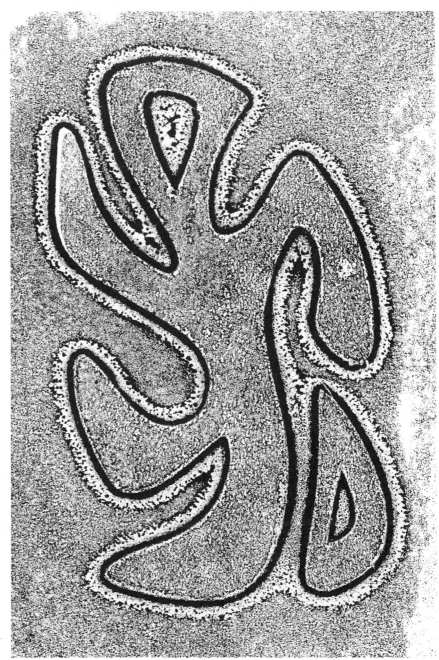

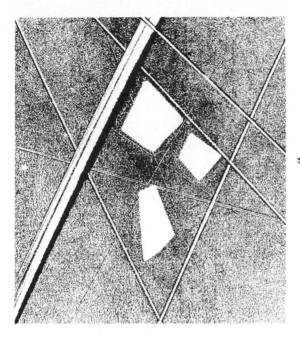

Still using the inked-up glass sheet, draw into the ink as well as using masks. You can use a pencil-shaped piece of wood or a small piece of cardboard.

Prepare a drawing or pattern on thin paper. Place a blank piece of thin paper over the inked-up glass sheet. Place the drawing over that and, with a sharp pencil, trace over your drawing. Take care not to touch the paper too much. A wooden 'bridge' will help.

These monoprints were made by the method described. By pressing the finger gently as you trace, areas of ink can be transferred as well as the line. Newspaper photographs can be traced to make monoprints this way.

Materials required for stencil.

Stencil and mask.

Chalk and powder stencil.

Counter change print patterns
from cardboard blocks.

Print from hessian, textured
wallpaper and card.

Two colour print from cardboard.

Print from india rubber block (eraser).

Cut stencil design stippled with brush and coloured inks.

Head made up from coloured newsprint.

Felt tip pen and
coloured inks on
sandpaper.

Suitable pattern for working in
sand.

Natural coloured sand on glue
brushed design.

A transfer print from
laminated plastic.
A spoonful of paint mixed
with washing-up liquid
and water is brushed onto
the plastic surface.
Patterns are best made
with the fingers or pieces
of card. Paper is laid over
the paint and lightly
rubbed with the palm of
the hand and then pulled
off. The over and under
pattern is characteristic of
this print.

The roller itself can be used to make prints. A paper shape placed under the paper will add another effect.

Textured paper, card, hessian and string can be cut out and stuck down to make a block. This can be inked over and several prints taken from it.

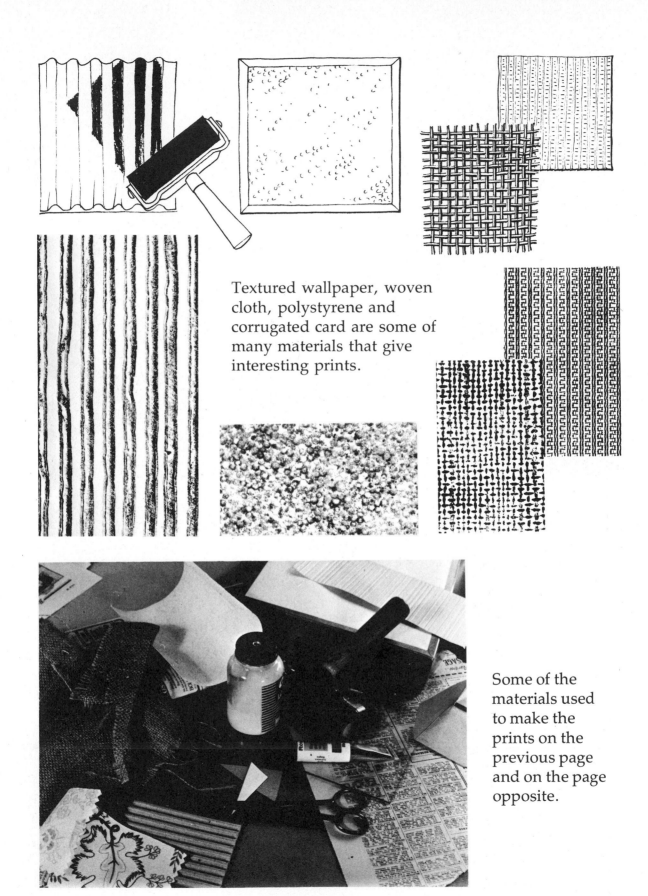

Textured wallpaper, woven cloth, polystyrene and corrugated card are some of many materials that give interesting prints.

Some of the materials used to make the prints on the previous page and on the page opposite.

Latex adhesive brushed onto a card background makes a printable surface when dry.

Small card cut-outs print black – lines scored into card stay white.

See what happens when you build up a cardboard block by sticking extra bits on.

The block for this print is made by covering cardboard with Universal adhesive, then scraping a design with a card comb. When dry the block is inked or painted over and a print taken from it.

In this case the printing medium is white poster paint on black paper.

Two-colour prints

Use two different-coloured printing inks and two blocks. Black and red perhaps. Make a careful drawing of what you want to print, using two colours. Trace all the black bits and transfer them to cardboard or a plastic tile. Do the same with the coloured bits. Make several prints from the coloured block. Overprint with the black block taking care to line it up properly.

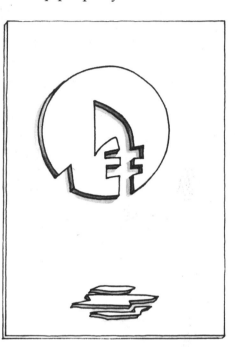

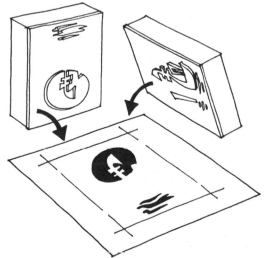

If you hold a plastic tile under the hot tap it will soften and be easier to cut with scissors. It will last much longer than cardboard.

Offset printing

Dab printing ink onto something like a nail or staple. Roll a soft rubber roller or a piece of rubber pipe lagging over the staple. The print is now on the roller. Roll the roller over a piece of paper and the print will transfer to the paper.

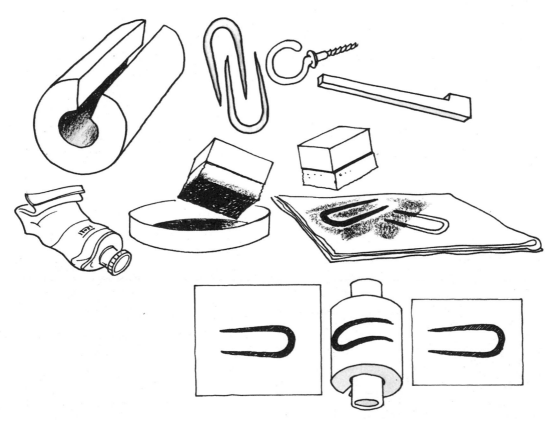

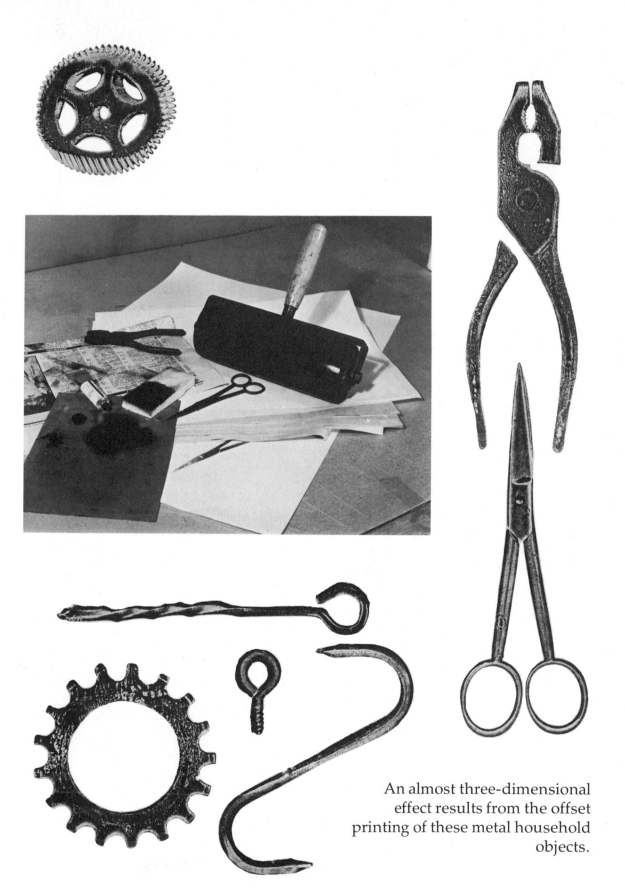

An almost three-dimensional effect results from the offset printing of these metal household objects.

The beach is the place for sand art. A rake makes parallel lines and can be used for straight or curved lines. A bucket for cutting circles in the sand as well as making sand pies, and a spade for short straight marks. You think of other things for making impressions in the sand.

Raking patterns round rocks is a well-known Japanese art form.

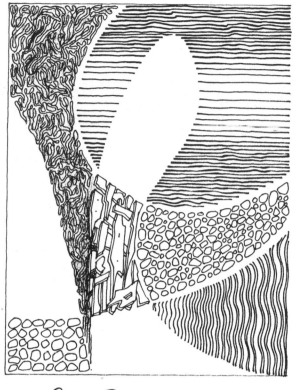

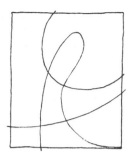

Scratch a series of lines in the sand to make a number of forms. Fill in the forms with anything you can find on the beach. Seaweed, pebbles, driftwood, shells, etc. Leave some forms bare and rake others to make a contrasting design. Boxes and plastic cups make different sand pies.

Sand can sometimes be found in different natural colours.

Ordinary sand can be dyed by soaking it in ink and allowing it to dry.

Draw a design using a paste stick or brush and glue. Sprinkle sand over glue and shake off surplus.

Geometric patterns are good for this sort of sand art. If you use two or more colours allow one to dry before putting on the next.

This Sand pattern was designed by American Indians from Colorado. It represents the seeds and fruits from the four corners of the Earth.

You can use emery paper and fine and coarse
sandpapers to make a sand-textured collage. Colour the
sandpaper with transparent inks.

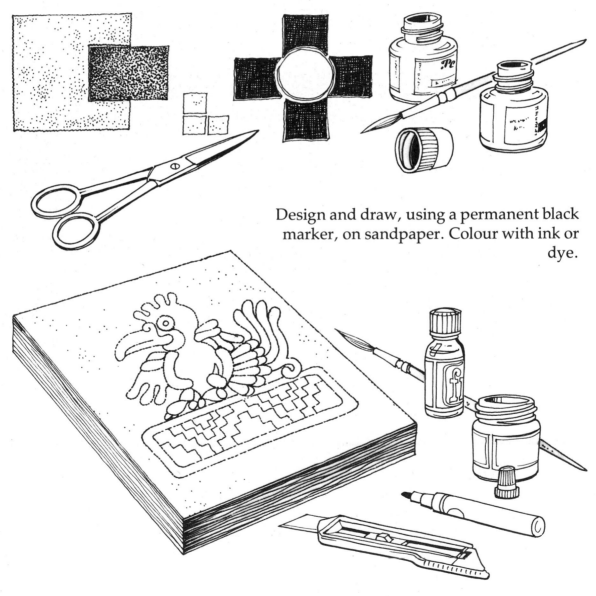

Design and draw, using a permanent black
marker, on sandpaper. Colour with ink or
dye.

The patterns in the sand are changed by the sea water washing over them. Sometimes the water runs in channels making patterns of light and shade. You can achieve a similar effect by trickling water onto sand in a tray. But the real thing is best. Use it as an idea for a design. This was made by painting grey rivulets on black paper, stippling all over with white paint, then adding shadows and highlights.

A mono-stencil. It can only be done once. Sprinkle dry sand on white paper. Brush paths through the sand with a water-colour brush. Spray or stipple black paint over the sand. When dry shake off sand.

A. Sprinkle sand on paper

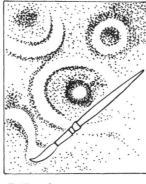

B. Brush patterns

C. Spray over sand

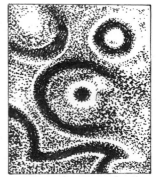

D. Shake off sand when dry.

Ink, wax and paper

Marbling patterns

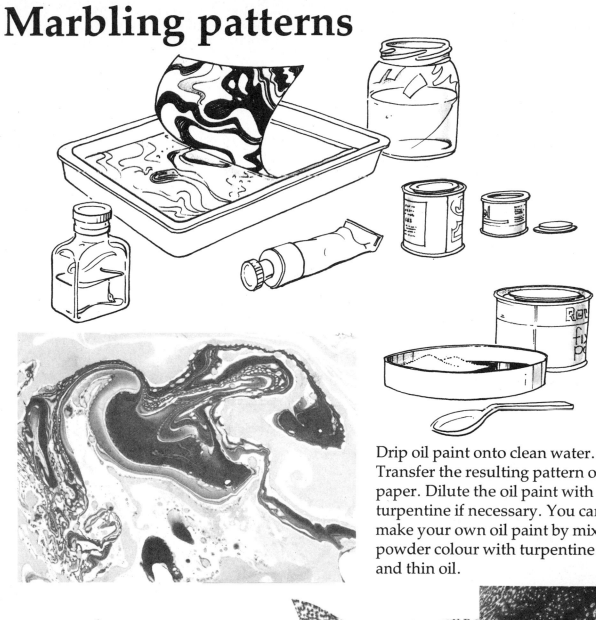

Drip oil paint onto clean water. Transfer the resulting pattern onto paper. Dilute the oil paint with turpentine if necessary. You can make your own oil paint by mixing powder colour with turpentine and thin oil.

Use cellulose paint from an aerosol spray on water to get these results. Work quickly or the cellulose becomes skin-like. Make sure the room is well ventilated as the fumes are not good for you.

Use your marbling patterns for collages.
Some patterns are particularly suitable
for sea, cloud or landscapes. Add detail
with pen or brush if it seems worth while.

You can mask the paper with
cut-out shapes *before*
transferring a marbling
pattern. It's best to use an
adhesive that can be peeled
off, like Spraymount or
Latex.

Mix wallpaper paste in a flat dish.
2 teaspoons to 1 pint of water.

Draw stick backwards and
forwards across surface.

Drip oil paint onto surface.

Transfer pattern
onto paper.

A plastic seed tray
makes a good dish.
Some patterns make
good backgrounds
for drawings and
paintings.

Experiment with
two colours and
thinner or thicker
paint.

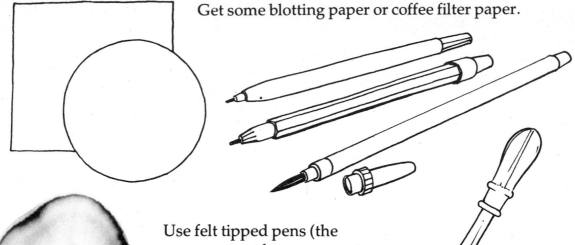

Get some blotting paper or coffee filter paper.

Use felt tipped pens (the pens *must not* be permanent – most felt tips are soluble) to draw several rings like a target. Drip water slowly at the centre.

Draw simple shapes on blotting paper. Lay on water for 2 seconds. Tear or cut blotting paper up and form a collage. This can be done wet or dry.

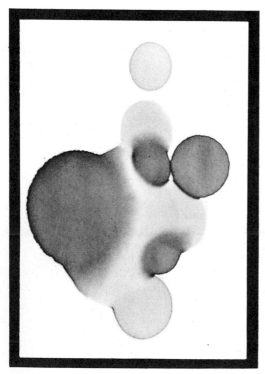

Ink and water dripped onto blotting paper.

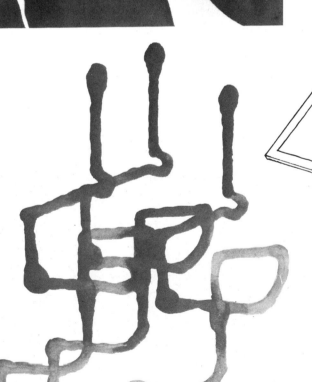

Oil or candle grease dripped onto blotting paper will resist ink or water colour. Candle grease can then be cracked off when completely dry.

An ink run pattern is made by putting a few drops of ink onto a sheet of card and tilting and moving the card. An unusual repeat pattern is made by putting several drops down and then tilting and rotating.

Rub damp cotton wool onto card or paper leaving dry areas. Ink is then touched lightly to the wet areas. The handle end of a brush can be used for the inking. If the ink does not spread quickly, add one drop of washing-up liquid to the ink bottle.

Prints from card tubes and edges on wet and dry paper.

Brush Latex adhesive in a few bold strokes over white card. When this Latex is dry (½ hour) brush over with ink – any sort. When this is dry, rub off the Latex.

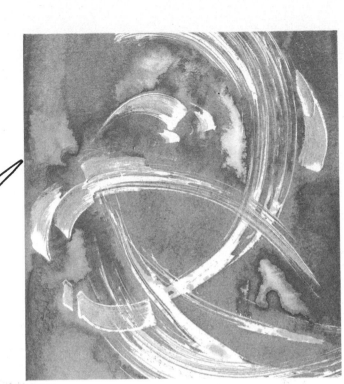

Stick paper strips temporarily to a background and over-paint with paint, ink or crayon. So that the masking strips can be removed easily, stick them with Spraymount (a temporary mounting adhesive) or small dots of Latex adhesive.

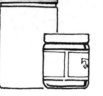

A drop of paint can be blown to form tree- and root-like shapes. Use a plastic straw for blowing.

Blot patterns without a fold. Use thick poster paint on a sheet of polythene. Fold and press the paint into shape. Open. Transfer onto a sheet of paper.

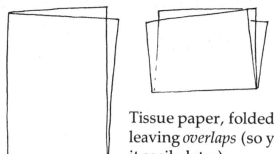

Tissue paper, folded twice. Fold leaving *overlaps* (so you can unfold it easily later).

Brush a little water onto the folded tissue. Brush ink and dab onto paper. Unfold carefully.

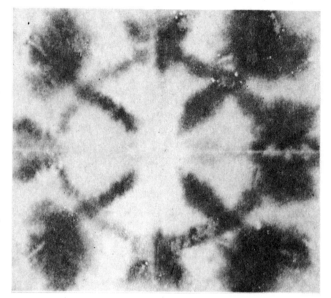

Cut tissue and ink on damp paper.

29

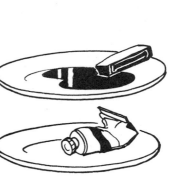

Oriental brush and ink stick.
Lamp black can be used instead.
Hold brush upright and move
whole arm.

White chalk
rubbed onto grey
card. Brush
strokes in lamp
black.

Cat painted with
clear water.
Chinese ink
applied with
edge of brush.

Paint design with water. It is best to paint a little at a time. Touch ink to wet area.

Experiment with two colours within the same area. See colour picture on Page **2**.15

Black and diluted ink. Paint slowly and *continuously*. Don't stop when painting a form or you'll get tide marks!

For sharp lines, let one feature dry before painting another over it. The spots on the dark pig were made by allowing drops of water to fall on the dried ink and then blotting them with blotting paper.

Rub candle wax to and fro over white card. Apply ink
with cotton wool.

Draw with white
wax crayon or
candle.

Brush over with ink.

When one coat of ink
has dried you can ink
over again in selected
places.

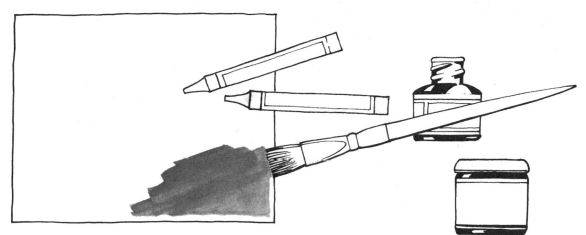

Wax scraper-board

Scribble with light-coloured wax crayon onto white card. Paint all over with black indian ink. The ink covers more easily if you add a little black poster paint.

When dry, scrape your design, using sharpened edges of blocks of wood or a wood stylus.

Wax transfer

Cover white paper with
white chalk – rub in well with finger. Over that, draw wax crayon lines.
Use two or more colours. Reverse paper onto a blank sheet of white or coloured
paper and draw a picture or pattern using wooden stylus or pencil.

Card tilt pattern. Poster paint and water.
Blown paint, using drinking straw.

Water design with
dripped ink.

Pig pattern. Soluble ink.

Chinese brushes
and ink for
oriental art
forms.

Poster paint.
Butterfly fold blot.

Poster paint
and stencil
brush over
masking
strips.

Chinese brush
and ink on
damp card.

Wax and ink scraper board
design.

Wax crayon and chalk
transfer.

Tissue paper and ink
fold pattern.

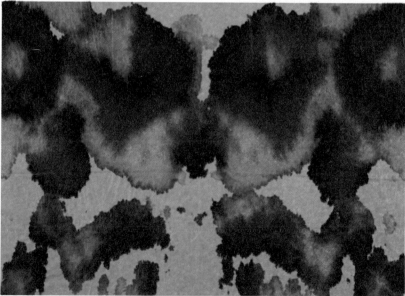

Card fold creatures. Light card and felt tip pens.

Paper straws. Cutting, pressing and bending.

Transferring newsprint

Cut pictures, lettering or words from newspaper. Rub candle wax over newsprint. Reverse onto plain paper and rub with thumb-nail or bowl of spoon.

Make an impression into thick cardboard using a wood stylus. It should be at least 1 mm deep. Place a sheet of thin paper over the top and rub with wax candle or crayon. Now brush ink over the rubbed wax.

Molten wax pictures. (When someone grown up is ironing!) Scrape tiny pieces of wax crayon onto a piece of paper that has been folded and opened. Use 2 or 3 colours. Refold. Ask mother to iron the folded paper. Put lots of newspaper underneath and a piece between the iron and the folded paper.

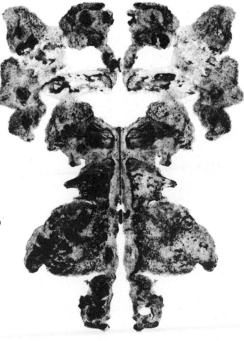

Ask your mother to iron a piece of card for you so it is warm. Draw on it with wax crayons.

PAPER

Cut tissue paper can be overlapped to produce different tones. It's easier to cut if you fold it between ordinary paper. Clear gum or wallpaper paste is best to stick it down.

Overlapping different colours of tissue is effective.

Different weights of paper can be cut into shapes and stuck down to make a collage.

Some magazine illustrations lend themselves to particular picture forms.

A surrealist picture. The pieces were put together from cut out magazine illustrations.

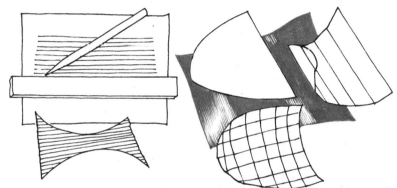

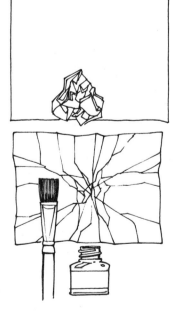

Score or fold card to give it a different texture. Crumple paper and unfold, brush ink over it, then wipe off the surplus ink. Try using these together with matt and gloss paper in a collage.

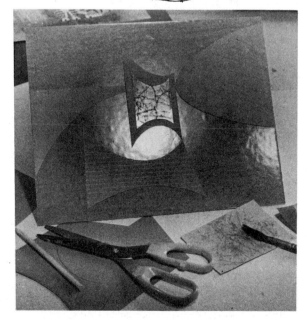

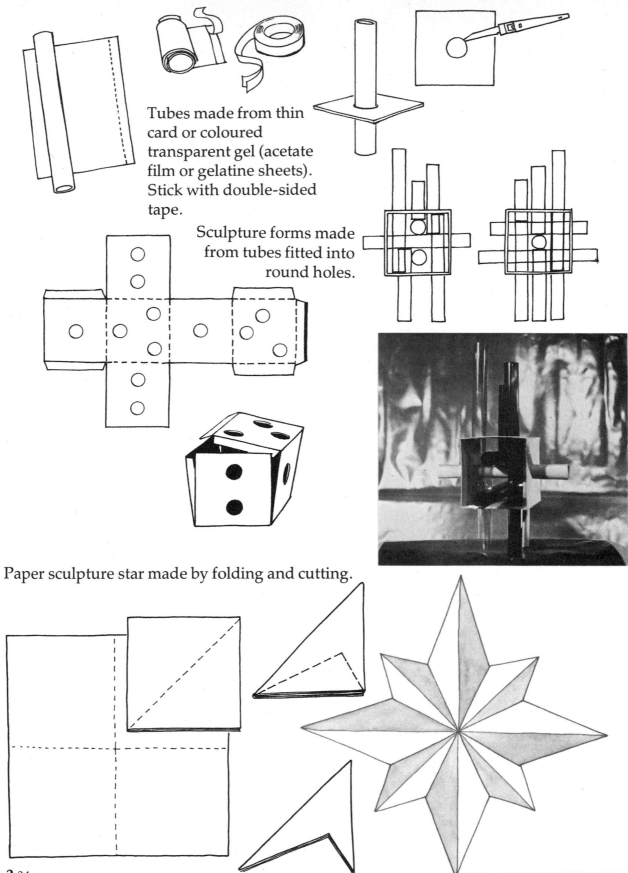

Tubes made from thin card or coloured transparent gel (acetate film or gelatine sheets). Stick with double-sided tape.

Sculpture forms made from tubes fitted into round holes.

Paper sculpture star made by folding and cutting.

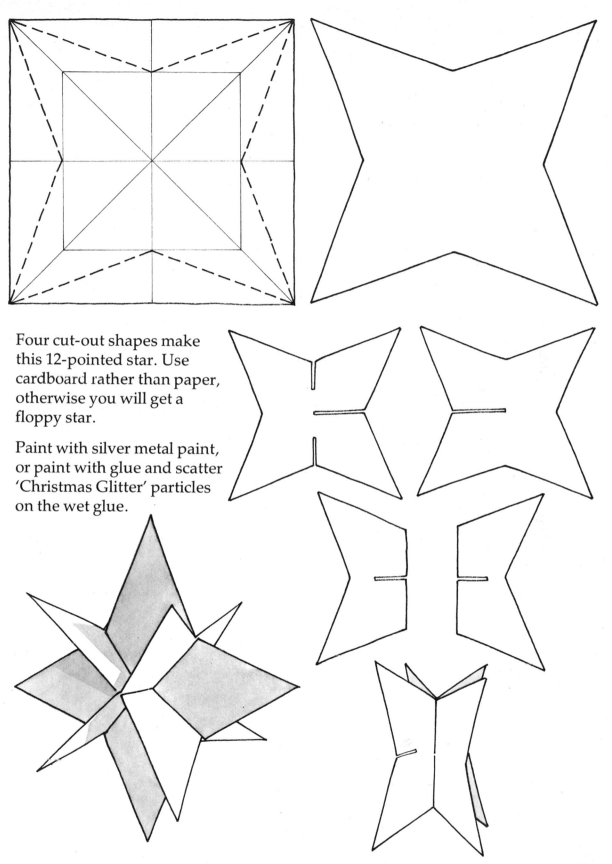

Four cut-out shapes make this 12-pointed star. Use cardboard rather than paper, otherwise you will get a floppy star.

Paint with silver metal paint, or paint with glue and scatter 'Christmas Glitter' particles on the wet glue.

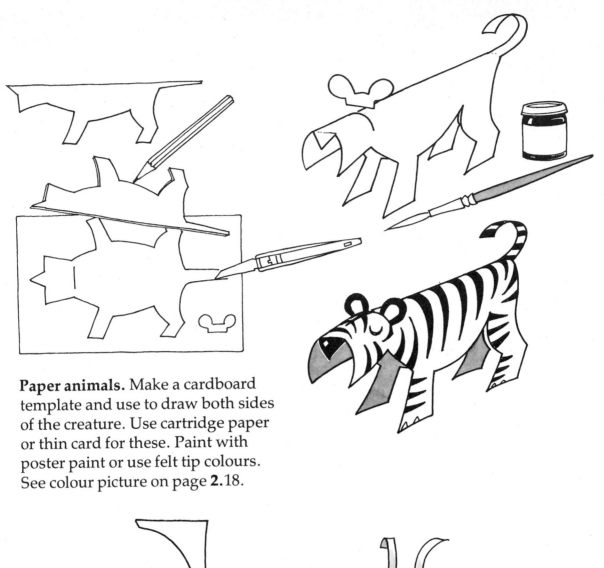

Paper animals. Make a cardboard template and use to draw both sides of the creature. Use cartridge paper or thin card for these. Paint with poster paint or use felt tip colours. See colour picture on page **2**.18.

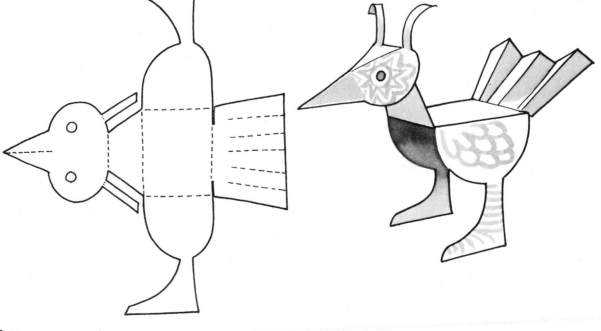

This sort of paper sculpture needs good quality cartridge paper. Use a sharp craft knife for cutting and scoring. If anything needs to be stuck down, use small spots of Latex adhesive. The paper sculpture should be mounted on coloured card to set it off. Never paint the cartridge paper. The interest is in the crisp paper forms and the shadows resulting from the relief forms.

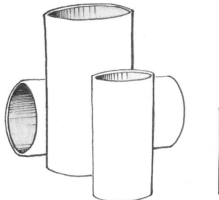

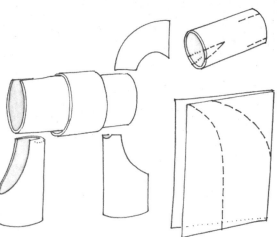

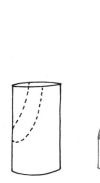

Toilet roll centres or cardboard tubes are used to make the body, legs and head of this horse; thin card for the neck and tail.

Free-standing forms are made by slotting the two cut-out pieces together.

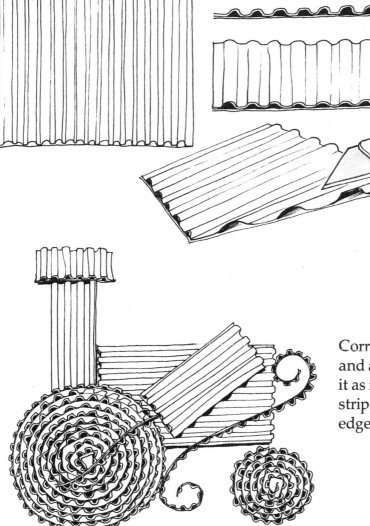

Corrugated card makes unusual and attractive paper sculpture. Use it as flat cut-out shapes, or cut it in strips, roll it and use it standing on edge.

When cutting use a craft knife or scissors. The angle at which you cut corrugated card makes a difference to the pattern of the edge.

The craft knife should be sharp, otherwise the cut edge of the corrugated card will fray and look messy. But be careful not to cut your fingers, or ask an adult to do the cutting for you.

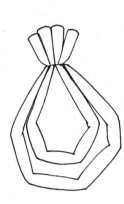

Art straws

Paper straws – not plastic – can be cut, stuck and tied to make unlimited shapes and patterns. If you are colouring the straws it's best to paint a lot of them with different-coloured poster paint before they are cut.

Wood sculpture
(free standing)

With a tenon saw, sandpaper and a supply of wood off-cuts you can create the most satisfying constructions. You will find that many scrap pieces of wood need nothing more than sandpapering. Others you may wish to cut to a different shape. Wood stains are obtainable for colouring. A tube of impact adhesive will do all the sticking necessary.

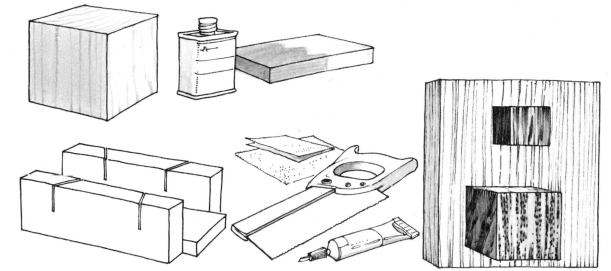

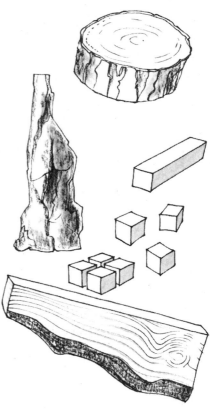

Wood sculpture (Wall plaque)

Choose a wooden baseboard with
an interesting grain. It is cheaper to
use a wood laminate. Find pieces of
wood with differing textures: bark,
log sections and small pieces cut
from wood dowling. It's the placing
of the pieces that makes the
picture. Don't stick them down
until you are satisfied.
Wood bark and timber form a
landscape with pressed leaves
forming a treescape.

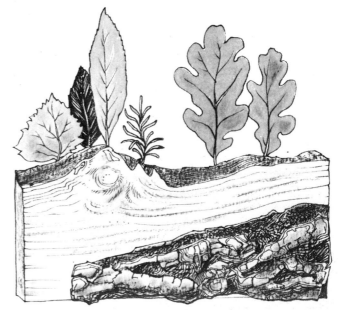

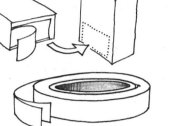

Polystyrene is useful for all sorts of shapes and forms. Carefully cut with a craft knife or saw it with a bread knife, or mark out your pattern and get an adult to do the cutting for you. You can buy an electric hot wire which cuts by melting the plastic.

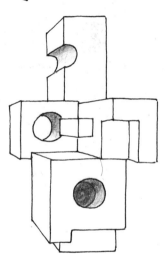

Polystyrene packing often looks like modern sculpture. If sticking polystyrene use a multi-purpose adhesive that will not melt the polystyrene.

For Wood, use a clear, quick-drying modelling cement for sticking, or double-sided sticky tape.

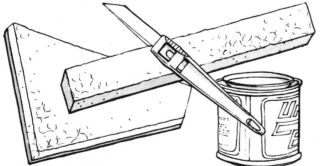

Polystyrene plaque

Polystyrene ceiling tiles and off-cuts are used to put together this lightweight wall plaque. It is important to use a light, sharp craft knife to cut polystyrene otherwise you will get a crumbly edge. Ask an adult to do the cutting for you. Many adhesives melt the plastic so use a universal adhesive to do the sticking.

Metal, light
and patterns

METAL

The Owl Family – print from metal

It's worth collecting small metal objects from which to make prints. The varying shapes of washers, nuts, staples and nails lend themselves to imaginative prints. A piece of foam rubber, soaked in water-based printing ink, is ideal for inking up the metal.

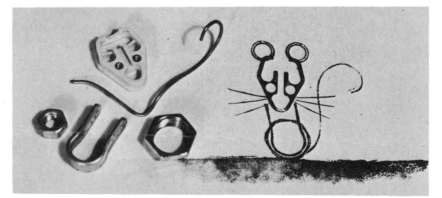

Nail collage

Some nails with interesting heads suitable for making a collage.

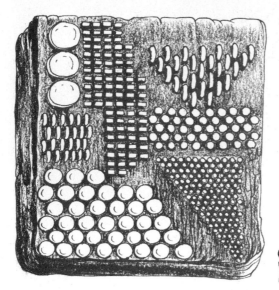

Choose a wood base that will not split when a great number of nails are hammered into it. You can drill suitable holes first, which will prevent splitting, or use cork. An old cork bathmat or several tablemats stuck together will do. Cork found on beaches is also good.

Metal foil, oven foil and silver paper are useful for making collages.

Moveable profile from coin and key chain

Metal assemblage

Viking ship from metal foil, nails, cup hooks and paper fasteners. The background is oven foil. Cut foil with old scissors. Foil can be scored to create lines and angles.

For heavier metal cutting use tin shears, wire cutters and a hacksaw. Ask an adult to help you with cutting and sawing, and beware! – when tin is cut it has *very* sharp edges. Wire profiles can be bent from coat-hangers and mounted on a wooden block.

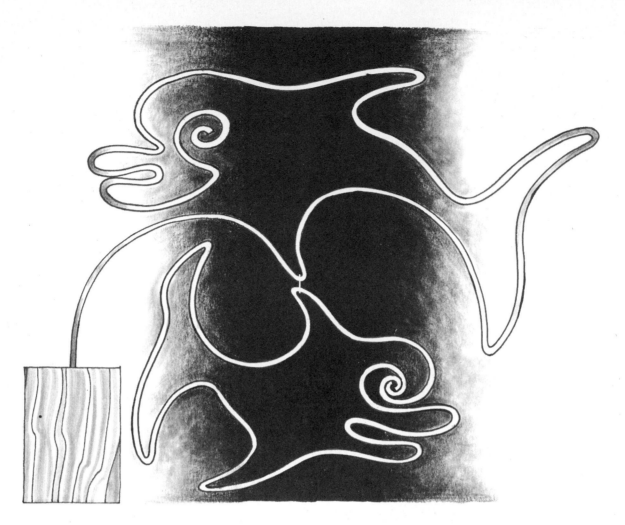

Dolphins shaped from coat-hanger wire.
Straighten the wire first and clean with a
household abrasive to make the metal shine.

Two lengths of galvanised wire bent in gentle
curves to form a sculpture. The four ends are
planted in four holes in a wood block. For a really
beautiful wire sculpture use 4 mm copper wire.
You buy it in rods approximately 2 metres long.

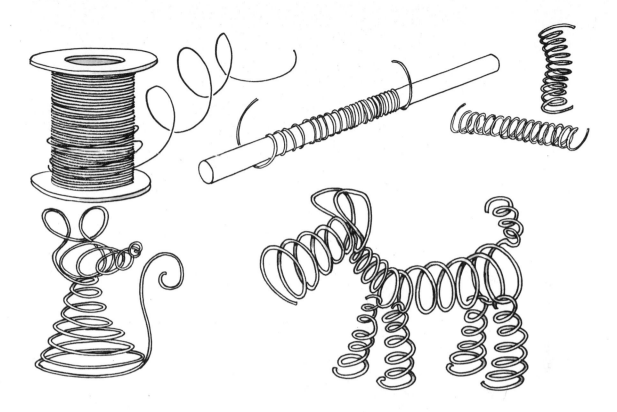

Wire sculpture

Plastic-coated wire and florists' wire can be used to shape free-standing figures. Fine wire can be crumpled and used like clay to shape forms.

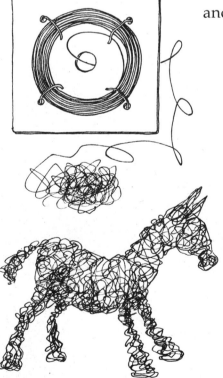

Chicken wire can be obtained with various sizes of mesh. It is generally galvanised and rust proof.

The hexagon is a six-sided shape. It provides an interesting pattern when interlocked and forms cubes when overlapped.

Crumpled and moulded by hand, chicken wire can be used to create three-dimensional forms.

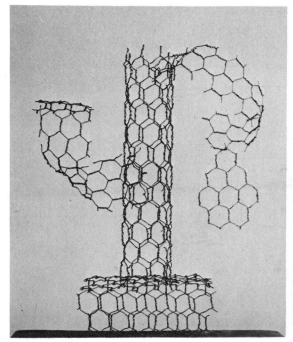

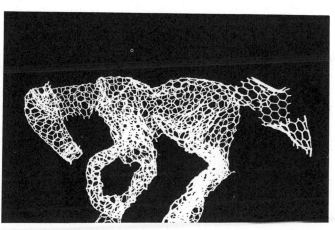

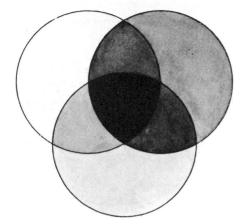

Transparent designs

Overlapping transparent material brings about new forms and new tones or colours. The three primary colours, red, yellow and blue, when overlapped show seven colours. See colour picture on page **3.16**.

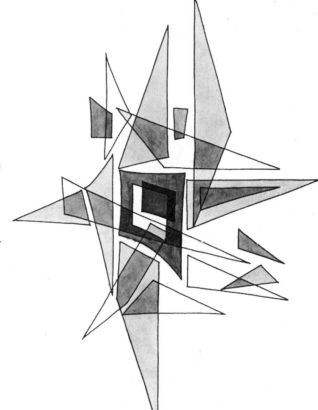

Coloured gels (acetate film or gelatine sheets) are used in theatre lighting. A collage made by overlapping scraps of these is effective if stuck on transparent material and placed in the window or with a light at the back. Stick with all-purpose clear adhesive.

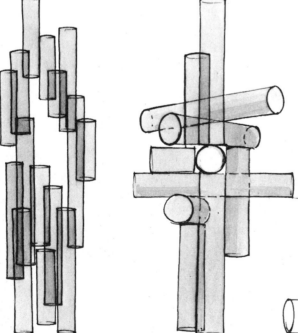

Gels rolled into tubes can be stuck with double-sided adhesive tape. Stuck to each other you can design a transparent tubular structure.

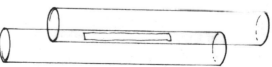

Cartoons and backgrounds

Acetate film is a clear, transparent material used by cartoon film animators. Draw with indian ink on one side. Turn over and colour with acrylic or poster paint. This ensures that the black outline is sharp. The ink drawing should be traced from your original pencil drawing which can be quite rough.

Your painted drawing on film can now be placed over various backgrounds. Here are two drawn textured backgrounds and a photograph.

Shiny relief pictures

Design a picture or pattern that can be cut out and stuck down on card so that all the bits are raised about 1 mm. You can add detail by scoring grooves into the card bits with a sharp piece of wood – not too sharp or it will tear the card.

Paint over the entire picture with matt black paint, poster colour or emulsion. When the paint is quite dry rub over with a soft cloth. Where you rub, the paint will shine. For a metallic shiny finish there is a metal paint in tubes that you can rub on, then polish.

Cover every bit with matt black paint.

Rub the metallic paint on with your finger.

Windows and light

Try exploding a simple shape like this. The design can be used as an unusual window. Coloured paper or 'gel' should be stuck on the back of these window designs. Painting the front of the window with a mixture of emulsion paint and sand gives it an appearance of stone. Do this before you stick the coloured material on the back.

Circular windows can be designed by folding and cutting paper first.

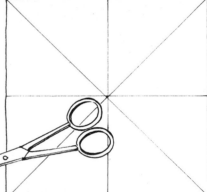

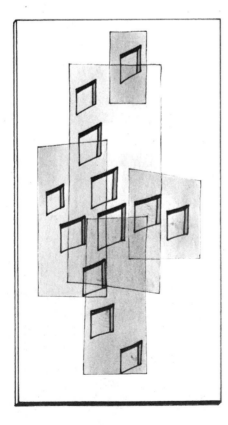

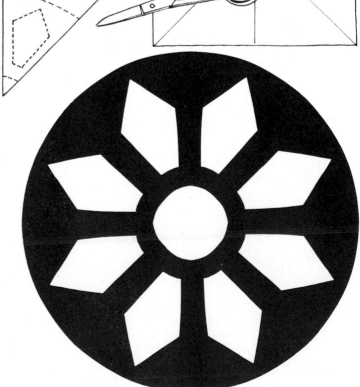

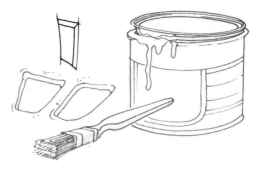

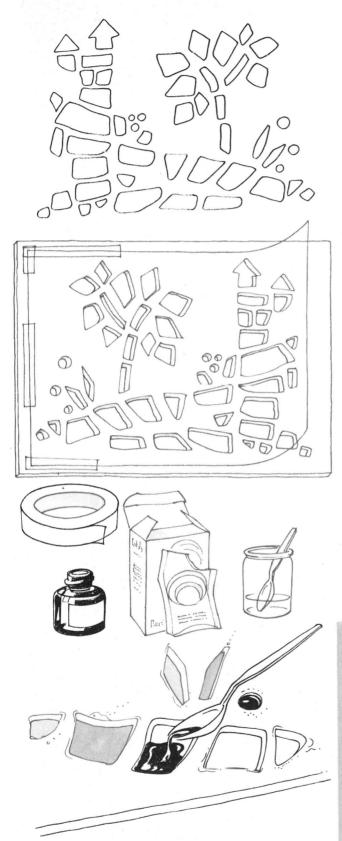

Simulated stained glass

Continuing the window theme, design a picture like a simple mosaic on thick card. Cut out all the shapes. Paint the card with sand-textured paint. When dry, reverse the card and stick clear acetate film to the back. This can be done with double-sided or ordinary clear adhesive tape.

Make up a very stiff gelatine mixture using household gelatine. About one teaspoon of gelatine to 2 teaspoons of hot water. When the gelatine has dissolved, mix in a few drops of coloured ink – ink, not paint. When it cools and starts to set, pour it into the window depressions. Use as many colours as you wish. The result looks like very thick coloured glass.

Decorated foil

Metal foil can be engraved by drawing into the surface with a wooden stylus. Put a few newspapers under the metal foil to protect the table and to obtain a deeper groove. Left this way the design will be sunken. Turn the foil over and the design will be raised.

You can paint the foil with black poster paint and, when dry, rub it with fine sandpaper. It gives the whole thing an antique look!

Try taking a wax crayon rubbing from the design.

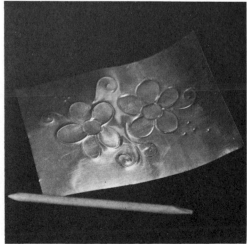

Foil figures

Foil of this sort can be cut from the containers used in Chinese and Indian "take away" meals. A collage using cut and scored foil is shown against a background of rough hessian and corrugated card. The contrast between rough and smooth is always effective.

The chessman figure and bull are made by folding and rolling the flat sheet of foil after cutting it. When curving foil, do it by rolling it against something round otherwise you will get a series of crinkles.

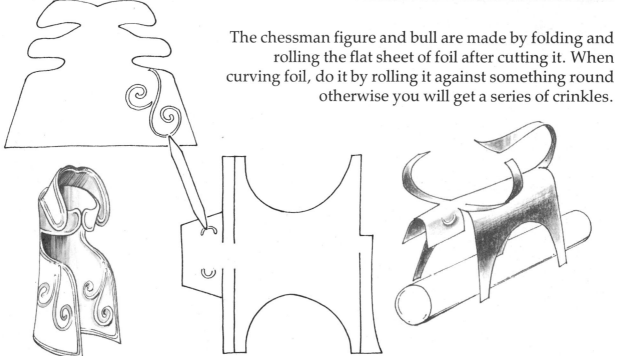

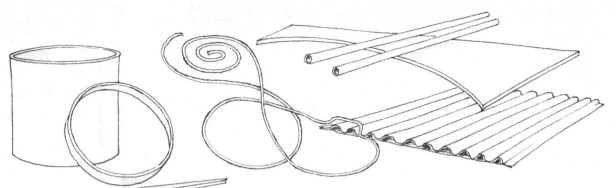

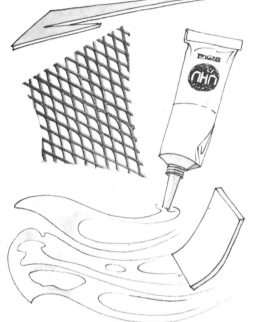

Simulated metal relief

You can make anything look like metal by covering it with metal paint. Even bits of rubbish can be transformed by doing this. The card background is covered with shapes cut from plastic netting, corrugated cardboard, drinking straws, a section of cardboard tube and bits of string. When a design emerges the bits are stuck down. Spilt glue makes its own pattern if you drag cardboard through it! Now paint it with metallic paint. This you can do with a brush and gold leaf paint or spray it with a metallic aerosol spray.

Metallic bits and pieces make light reflective collages and assemblages.

Dolphins from two wire coat hangers.

Drawing on transparent film can be positioned and repositioned over any sort of background.

Three primary colours overlap to make seven in all.

Coloured acetate film cut and overlapped to form a transparent collage.

Metallic paint on piped tube adhesive.

Burnished
metallic
paint
on card
relief
design.

(above) Cut paper mosaic. Light card and water colour.

(above right) Folded and cut black paper over ink splashed white card.

Beans and seeds stuck to thick cardboard.

Material collage. All pieces can be repositioned to alter design.

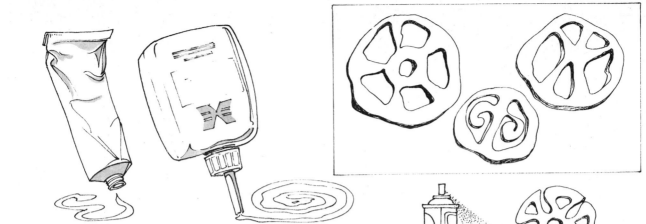

Simulated metal relief

Squeeze glue shapes onto card. Use Universal or contact adhesive. When dry, spray with black paint from one direction. Then spray with metallic paint from the other direction. Or simply paint with gold leaf paint. Cut shapes out and rearrange on a dark or bright coloured background. Metallic gold shapes look good against red card.

String

String patterns

A universal adhesive spread thickly on a card base will remain tacky long enough for a string pattern to be stuck down. It can also be used as a block from which to make a print.

With a complicated string pattern, use the adhesive in small areas and put the string down a little at a time.

The background can be painted card or hessian stuck on card.

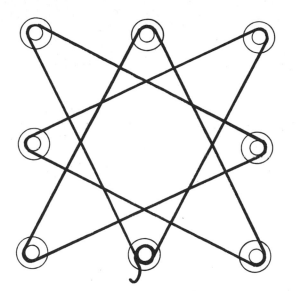

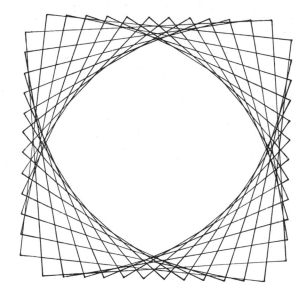

Geometric patterns can be made by wrapping string round a series of drawing pins or nails. The effect of curves can be made but only straight lines are used.

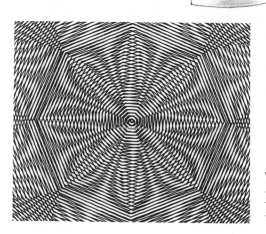

Pin a cardboard cut-out to a piece of card and trace the shape with a pen. Move the shape on and trace again. Repeat until a satisfying pattern is produced.

This pattern could be made by hand, given time. In this case a computer did the job in a fraction of the time.

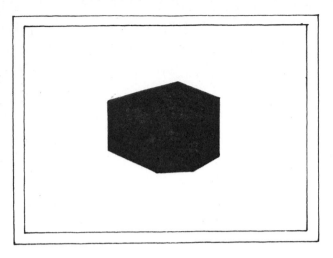

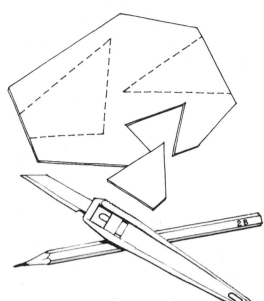

Reflected patterns

A shape cut from another shape and turned over brings about a reflecting pattern, the spaces being part of the pattern.

Cutting a shape into bits and moving the bits will bring about a design. This process is called 'exploding' because the pieces are moved outwards from the middle.

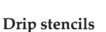

Drip stencils

Make a simple design by dripping washing-up liquid onto white card or paper. Spray paint over the design, or use a toothbrush and nail to stipple. The paint or ink must be permanent.

Drip more washing-up liquid to continue the design. Spray over again. Wash under tap and leave to dry.

Mobiles

The only difficulty about making a mobile is to make it balance. The suspended objects are best made from materials that can be added to or from which bits can be removed. Cardboard, art straws, tin foil do well. Plasticine is good but heavier.

Balance is achieved by moving the threads from which the mobile objects are suspended.

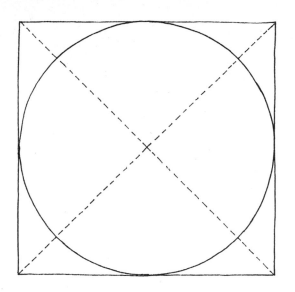

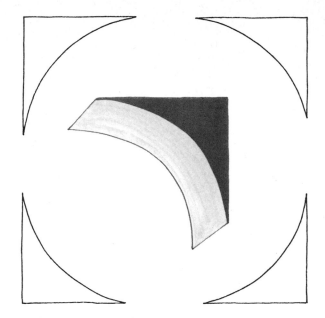

Repeat patterns

The simplest and most effective pattern is made from a circle and a square. Just one corner is used to make hundreds of patterns. Make a little block from polystyrene, wood, rubber or cardboard. Ink up from an ink pad and start printing. The examples have been used for floor tiles. See how many more you can make.

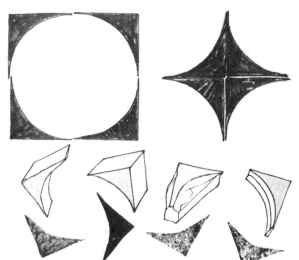

Relief panel

This relief panel is made by cutting two thicknesses of cardboard into small shapes and sticking them to a card background. The thickness of the pieces causes deep shadows and it's interesting to hold the finished work at different angles to the light to see the different effects. Paint it an overall matt white or light colour as this will give the most satisfying lighting effect.

Also suitable for metallic paint.

For use as a printing block.

From which to make a rubbing.

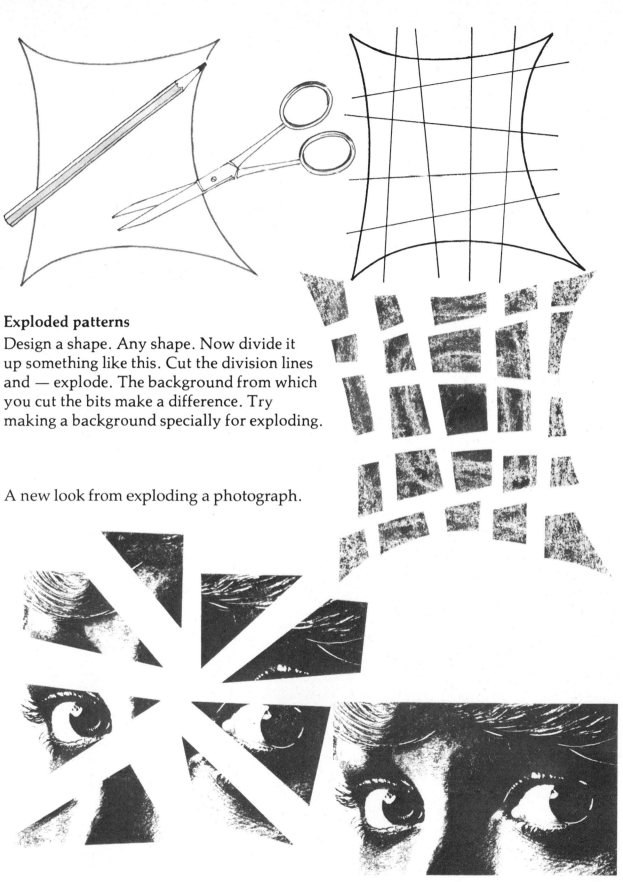

Exploded patterns

Design a shape. Any shape. Now divide it
up something like this. Cut the division lines
and — explode. The background from which
you cut the bits make a difference. Try
making a background specially for exploding.

A new look from exploding a photograph.

Paper mosaic

Colour cartridge paper with paint or ink. Use a coarse brush and allow the paint to streak a bit, let one colour run into another.

When dry, cut the paper into strips, and the strips into small squares. Don't make perfect squares! It's *not* being perfect squares that gives character to this sort of mosaic.

You can create a picture that is entirely covered with little squares (colour picture on page **3**.18) or do something like this.

Seeds and beans

Here seeds are used as units for a highly textured mosaic. This kind of work is most satisfying, though time consuming.

Choose about half a dozen different sizes, shapes and colours of seeds and beans. Stick them down onto a really thick piece of cardboard or hardboard. Use clear adhesive or multi-purpose glue. When sticking down large areas of small seeds, glue the whole area and try to get all the seeds down before it dries! The seeds that I find most useful are: black and white peppercorns, white haricot beans, lentils, split peas and sunflower seeds.

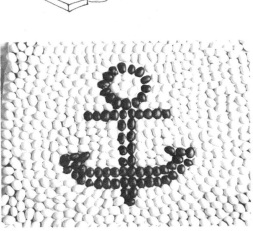

Pebbles and stone

Pebbles, worn smooth by the sea, are used to make paths. By using black and white pebbles, patterns are made. You could do the same thing with white beans. Paint beans black by putting paint and beans in a plastic bag and shaking them up. Plant the beans in modelling clay.

A Romano-British mosaic. About 9,500 pieces of stone are shown here.

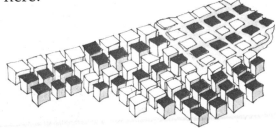

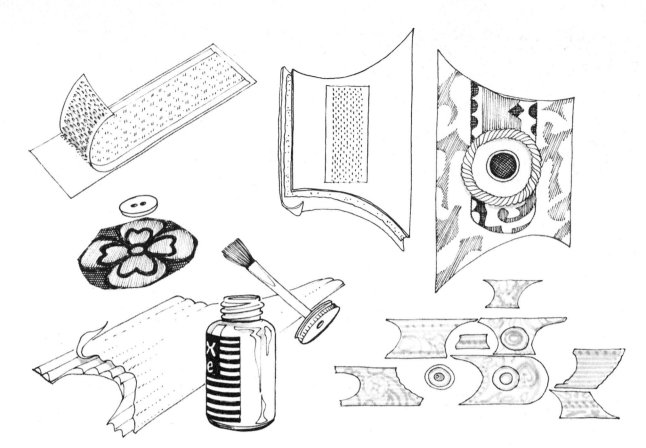

Material collage

When cloth and other fabrics are used in a collage it is useful to be able to reposition the pieces. Drapers' shops stock a tape that will attach itself to woolly materials but can be detached. Here I have used bits from the rag bag, stuck with latex adhesive to card, foam rubber and corrugated card bases. As a wall hanging you can alter the design whenever you like.

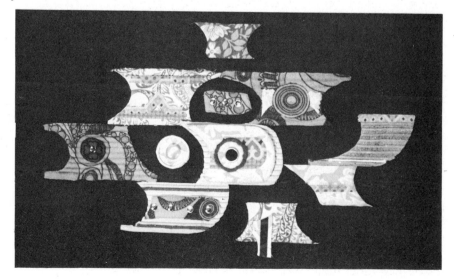

Patterns from bricks

Some complicated patterns emerge from both the two shapes and two colours. Most patterns are made from just the two shapes. The long shape – the stretcher, and the short shape – the header. You can design brick patterns by printing the individual brick shapes from a home-made block. Another method is to cut paper bricks and 'lay' them. Complicated patterns are best drawn in pencil first on a grid.

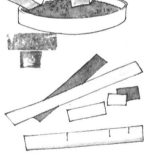

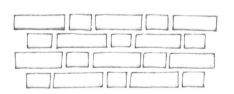

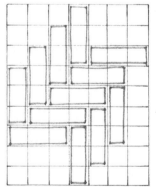

Rusty metal sculpture

This should only be undertaken with great care as cuts or scratches from rusty metal can be dangerous. If you want to try this it is a good idea to wear gloves. There is a lot of this scrap about. The texture and colour is often most satisfying. It can be cut easily with tin shears and stuck with epoxy resin adhesive. Brush away surplus rust particles with a wire brush. Varnish if you want it to shine.

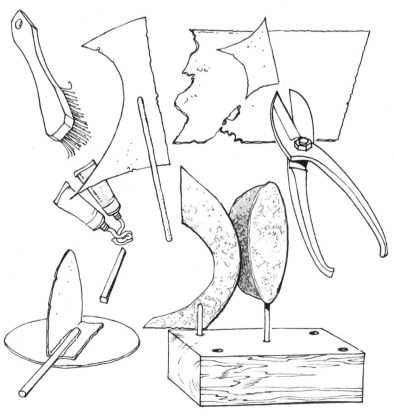

Real texture

Make up some wallpaper paste. On a suitable surface – a
laminated plastic top – lay a sheet of newspaper. Brush
paste all over it and put down a second sheet of
newspaper. Repeat this until you have a pile of six
sheets of newspaper, the top one pasted too. With your
fingers, push, prod and pull the newspaper until you
have produced a series of whorls and ridges. Leave to
dry. It takes some time with thick papier-mâché.

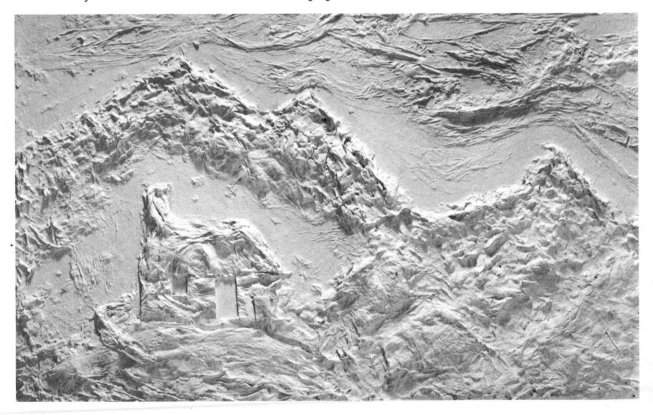

Stone, markers
and rubbings

Stone, clay and plaster

A collection of stone or pottery fragments can be assembled in the form of stylised creatures. Stick these down on thick card if your picture is to be hung.

Free-floating pieces look good in sand and can be re-assembled to make further patterns.

Smooth, water-worn glass is found on beaches. Usually it comes in all shades of green. Other colours are more rare. Stuck to transparent material they can be viewed with the light behind them. Use them to make abstract or representational patterns or designs. Pebbles of all sorts and colours are fun to play with. Of the millions and millions of pebbles, no one will ever be exactly like another.

You can draw on stones and pebbles with a felt tip pen.
The bird-headed man was drawn on stone in Easter
Island – not with a felt tip!

This bull's head was made in China 2,500 years ago. The
piece of flint, looking like a bull's head, was found in a
field last week.

Anything looks like a creature if you paint eyes
on it. Pebbles make excellent basic shapes on
which to work. You can also model creatures
from plasticine or use it to add bits to
something else.

Paving stone is often used to great effect on paths and patios. Broken or crazy paving can look most attractive; rather like a mosaic.

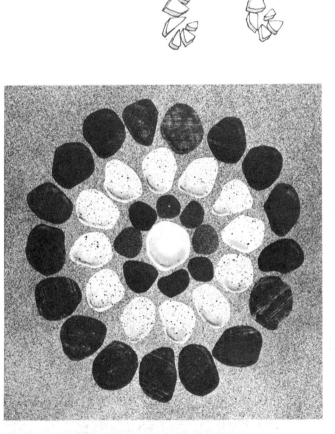

Collect pebbles in groups of different shapes, sizes and colours. They can be used to create all kinds of interesting patterns.

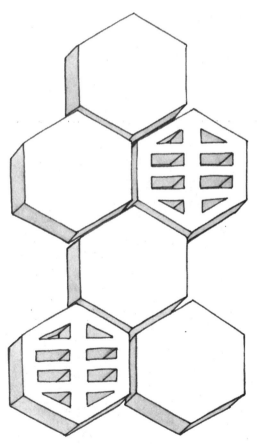

Councils often use concrete cast in shapes which can be put together to make patterns on pavements or shopping precincts.

Giant stones were used as temples long ago. You can still see them all over the country – Stonehenge is the most famous. You can use rockery stones in a similar way. Six stones, balanced, look very like a man. A simple and effective form of sculpture.

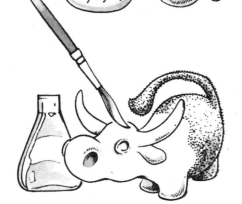

Clay or plasticine figures are best made by putting simple, round forms together. Then you can add detail. Objects like nuts and bolts, beads and buttons can be pressed into the clay. Try brushing glue over your model, then sprinkling sand on for a different texture.

Drinking straws make a prickly coat for a hedgehog.

Map pins make good eyes.

Clay or plasticine can also be used for impress patterns. Choose small household objects with interesting shapes that you can press into the rolled out clay. Clay will dry hard, plasticine will not. Before the clay dries (several hours) it could be cut into shapes and used as bricks or units for an assemblage.

Plasticine is excellent for plaster casts. Using the method of impress described, you can build a wall round the design and take a plaster of Paris cast from it. Always brush the mould with soapy water first. It makes it easier to remove the cast.

Plaster cast relief pattern of nails, bolts and electrical fittings.

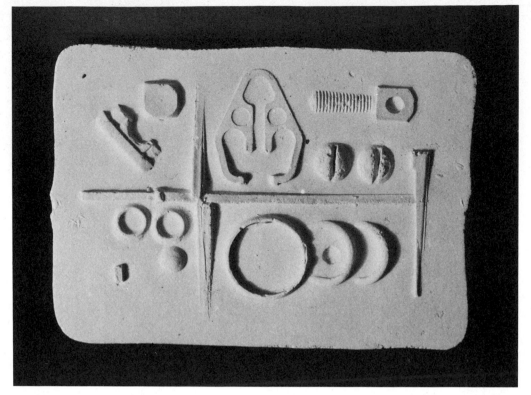

Make a cast of your own initial. Roll out plasticine like pastry. Use a hollow round object to cut out round pieces. Use a craft knife to cut out the letter. Put cut-out on another round piece and build a wall round it. A piece of wire pushed through the 'wall' will, later, act as something to thread a string through. Mix plaster and pour into mould. Allow to set, then remove. Pull the wire through the plasticine. Repair the wall before repeating the process.

Roman lettering incised in stone.

Stone carving, relief carving and sgraffito can be simulated, or actually done, on a flat plaster surface. Scrape away the dried plaster with a sharp metal point. A nail is very good. Draw in marker ink, or chalk, on the surface and scratch away. In the case of the owl, the plaster was painted with blue acrylic paint so the white plaster showed through when scratched.

Mix plaster with water to a workable, thick consistency and spoon onto a thick card. Using cardboard combs and edges, push the plaster about to form a picture.

It can be representational or simply a pattern of textures. When dry, (about an hour in a warm room) you can paint it over with waterproof ink. The ink runs in the plaster grooves, where it colours dark, but stays light on the raised plaster.

To add the finishing touch to the plaster panel, brush over with clear varnish.

Simulated cave art

This looks like a cave painting done 30,000 years ago. Actually it's black poster paint on a chunk of rockery stone. If you can't get any real stone, cover card with plaster and draw or paint on that. Another way of simulating cave art is to scratch on plaster with three nails.

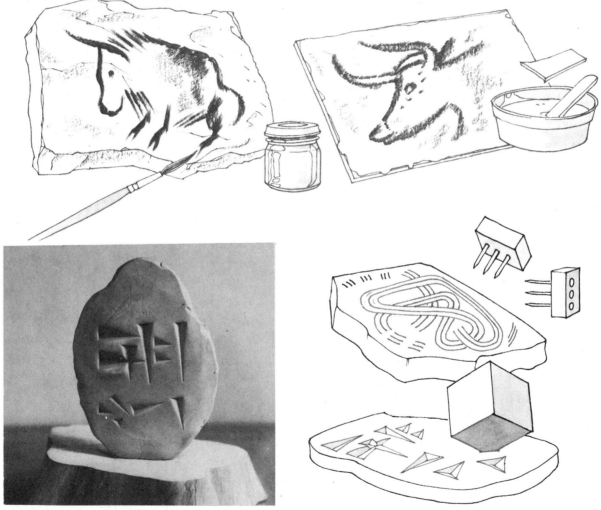

This is cuneiform writing. You can simulate it by pressing a wooden cube into clay, making triangles of varying size and shape. Part of the writing on the clay shown here means 'A Head'.

Pens, pencils, brushes and markers

You could get along perfectly well with just one pencil or a felt tip marker, but it is worth using the right thing for the right job. If you owned all the different drawing implements on the market you simply wouldn't have room to house them. Most of the art forms in this book haven't needed pencils or pens or markers, but now it's their turn. For the directional drawings in the book I've used, for the most part, only two sorts of pencil and one fine point marker with a nylon tip. The grey washes were painted with a fine point water-colour brush.

The Pen

Elizabeth R

With so many fibre tip pens about, we don't use nibs so much. The character of pen writing is brought about by the thicks and thins of the pen strokes. You can make a quill pen. Use turkey or goose feathers. Cut the tip as shown. Use very little ink or you'll just get blots. The first Queen Elizabeth of England used a quill and her signature looked like this.

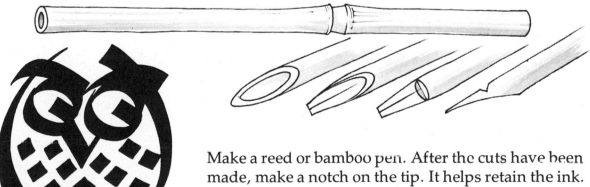

Make a reed or bamboo pen. After the cuts have been made, make a notch on the tip. It helps retain the ink. You can make really thick tips with bamboo.

Pencils come in two sorts. **B** for Black, which are soft, and **H** for Hard. There are over a dozen, ranging from 9H, Very Hard, to 6B, Very Soft. The soft pencils are good for rough drawing and for thick lines. Hard pencils are for detailed work and fine lines. You can buy white pencils, which are more like crayons, useful when drawing on tinted paper.

In the portrait you can see how the pencils have been used to outline and shade, and the white to highlight.

Wide brushes are good for painting large areas. You can lay a wash with water colour or with poster colour. Just slap it on. As the paint runs out the brush starts making texture. It can also be used like a wide pen. This sort of brush can be dabbed using the tip or the flat side to give the effect shown on the left.

If I don't use a fibre tip I use a fine brush for drawing cartoons; using Indian ink.

For larger areas of colour or grey tone I use a larger brush. These washes of water colour are put down quickly so that they dry without 'tide marks'!

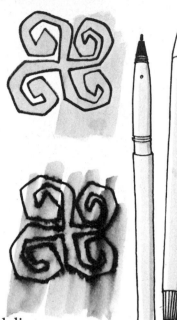

With markers there are two sorts of
ink and two sorts of tip. Felt tips for
bigger markers and fibre for smaller
ones. Some ink is permanent; you
can brush a wash over it and the ink
doesn't run. But other inks are
soluble. See what happens when
you brush over one of them!

When markers seem to be running out and the black line
goes rather grey and faint, don't throw them away. You
can use these markers to good effect, especially if you
use a paper mask. This picture was made with one new
marker and one old one.

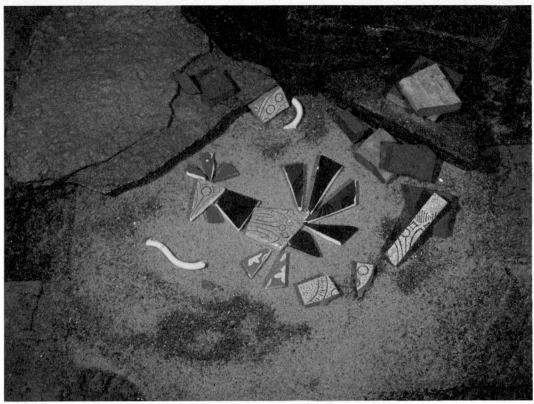

Stone, sand and pottery fragments . . . with a little imagination!

Paper, card, wax crayons and ink. All you need for making rubbings.

Rock, pebbles, water-worn glass and modelling clay.

Sgraffito.
Plaster of Paris is painted overall,
when dry the design is scratched
into the surface with a nail.

Black wax rubbing from plank,
cut out and stuck over red wax
rubbing from church pew.

Rubbing on tissue paper from cut
and assembled card design.

Two colour wax rubbing from dry glue whorl pattern. The rubbing then
brushed over with black ink.

Wax crayon
rubbing
from cut
and over-
lapped
paper, card
and wall-
paper.

This was made with just one black marker. The drawing
started with the sky and furthest part of the picture. I
chalked all over it with white chalk. Not wax crayon,
blackboard chalk. Rubbed in with the finger it stays on.
Then the next piece of drawing was done; chalked over,
and so on. The foreground is left pure black.

You could get the same effect by cutting out black paper
instead of using black marker ink.

If you wish you can fix each layer of chalk by using a
colourless fixative.

Marker ink penetrates paper. Turn the paper over and see what's come through. Different thicknesses of paper give a different result. Detail paper is too thin, cartridge paper too thick. Ordinary writing paper is what I used for this page of drawings.

RUBB -INGS

Rubbings

You can take a rubbing from anything that has a texture on it. Remember the engraved owl on page **4.7**? I put detail paper over it and rubbed with a black wax crayon. Where the plaster had been cut into, the wax had nothing to rub so it stayed white.

Woven paper produced a check pattern. Cardboard 'bricks' produced the pattern seen below.

A negative rubbing.

White paper on a plank of wood was rubbed with a wax candle. Cotton wool, soaked in ink, was rubbed all over the paper. The unwaxed parts took the ink, the wax wouldn't. When the paper is quite dry you can scrape away the wax with a craft knife blade if you want to.

Any colour ink or water colour can be used for these negative rubbings.

This black wax rubbing came from the wood grain of a pew in an old church.

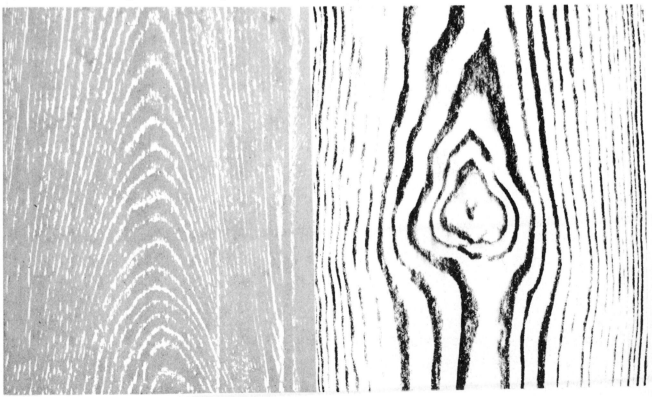

Wood grain rubbings can be cut up and used to make
pictures. An old piece of scrap timber can be marked
with scratch lines or nail holes so that the marks affect
the rubbing. Coloured wax rubbings can be used for part
of the picture. Do ask someone if it's all right before you
start hammering and scratching wood. Cardboard does
quite well instead.

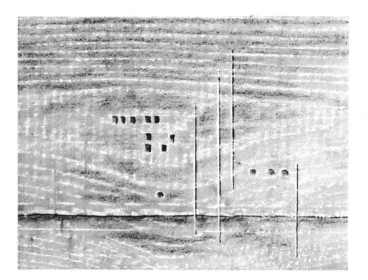

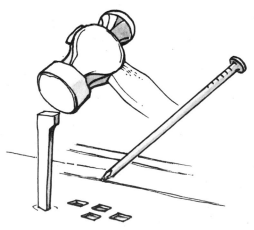

Rubbing from a simulated brass These are made from glass fibre and plastic and can be found at some Brass Rubbing Centres.

Brass rubbing

Most old churches have engraved brass and you may ask permission to make a rubbing. There will probably be a small charge. It is important to treat the brass carefully. Use a baby's hairbrush to brush away any dust, sand or grit from the brass. Fasten sufficient detail paper over the brass with masking tape and use proper heelball wax for the rubbing.

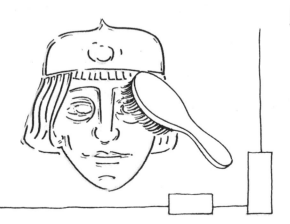

13th Century Monumental Brass and Rubbing

The brass is a miniature facsimile of that at Stoke D'Abernon, England.

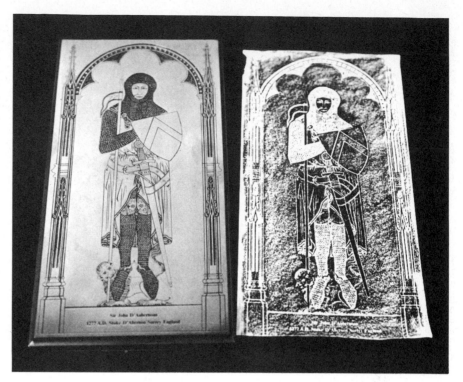

This is not a brass rubbing. After drawing my ancient knight, I cut him from paper, using textured wallpaper for the chain mail and cartridge paper for his face. A craft knife is best for the intricate cuts in eyes, nose and mouth. Then stick all the pieces down on card so they won't move when you do the rubbing.

An actual texture can be made by drawing into a thin film of Universal adhesive. Draw with a sharpened piece of wood. This makes tracks in the layer of adhesive.

When dry the ridges and tracks are hard and make an excellent surface for a rubbing.

The candle wax and ink method works well here. A colour version can be seen on page **4.18**.

Candlewax and ink rubbing.

Rubbing from cut pieces of corrugated card.

This landscape rubbing was made from cut paper of two thicknesses: writing and cartridge paper. They were lightly stuck to a sheet of card that had slight ridges on the surface.

The drawing shows which paper pieces were thick and which were thin.

See what happens when the papers overlap.

This is another rubbing from paper. The fighting cocks I saw in Thailand and I have based this design on a drawing I made. By cutting some parts of the design free, I could move them about until the whole thing appeared more active.

This design was based on Egyptian hieroglyphs. Instead of raising the surface, you draw into cardboard making furrows. The rubbing then comes out like this.

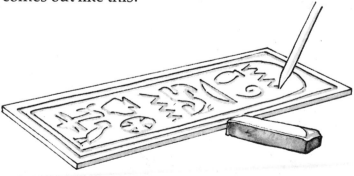

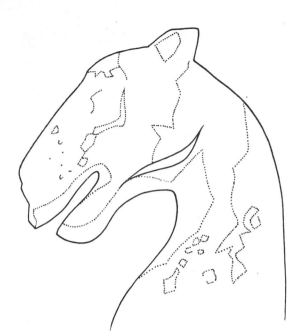

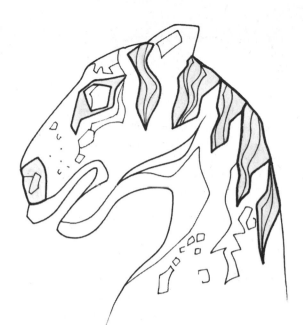

A stone Chinese horse was the inspiration for this rubbing. Cut out the shape first, then add some detail by scoring with a wooden point. Further cut out pieces are added and they, too, have been scored. The resulting rubbing has acquired rather subtle tones.

The frame to this picture is a rubbing from the back of a book! The whole thing was done on tissue paper, which is good for detail but wrinkles and tears easily.

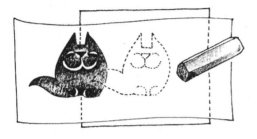

It is quite useful to take several rubbings from the same surface. When one is complete, move the paper and start again. Detail paper is thin enough to see what is underneath.

Here's a design that has been cut into pieces. The reason is so that you can move the shapes into different positions: a sort of cut-out animation. With the horseman and his steed, lots of horsemen could be made active in different ways in one picture.

At the top of the page are three Thai horses. (A rubbing from stone in Bangkok.) Below are our three horsemen with legs, arms and heads positioned in different ways so that more activity appears in the picture.

Here are all sorts of simulated textures: two sorts of wood grain, cloth that isn't cloth – it's paper with the pattern printed, something weird that looks like two figures and a vaulting horse – in fact it's a print from oven foil, an enlargement from a newspaper photograph. A volcano? No, it's a man's sleeve.

Effective abstract pictures can be made by rubbing away parts of photographs and newsprint.

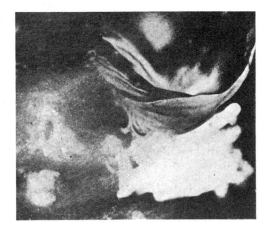

Dampen wire wool and rub gently on the area you want to erase.

Here's an old friend who has had part of his face most effectively removed by the wire wool method. An improvement?

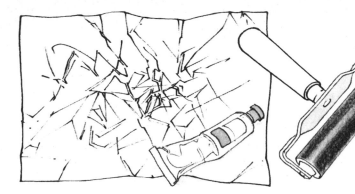

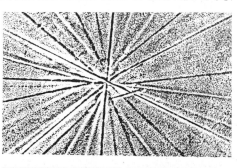

Greaseproof paper or tracing paper when crumpled makes a good texture from which to take a print. The best way to apply the ink is with an ink roller. Transfer the print by placing paper over the ink and rubbing.

Two similar prints, one from folded paper, the other from oven foil.

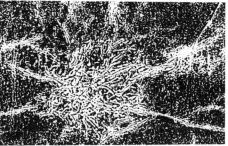

Make an elephant print by putting a stencil between the inked surface and the paper to which you transfer it.

Dye patterns

Dampen white card. Allow grains of cold water dye to fall on card. Drop gently on damp card for controlled patterns. Throw onto wet card for very active patterns. Drag wet grains with tip of brush for feathery effect.